My Emotions
Mes émotions

HAPPY
LA JOIE

A Crabtree Roots Book
Un livre de la collection Les racines de Crabtree

AMY CULLIFORD

Crabtree Publishing
crabtreebooks.com

School-to-Home Support for Caregivers and Teachers

This book helps children grow by letting them practice reading. Here are a few guiding questions to help the reader with building his or her comprehension skills. Possible answers appear here in red.

Before Reading:

- What do I think this book is about?
  - *This book is about feeling happy.*
  - *This book is about what feeling happy looks or feels like.*
- What do I want to learn about this topic?
  - *I want to learn what to do if I feel happy.*
  - *I want to learn what feeling happy looks like.*

During Reading:

- I wonder why...
  - *I wonder why we smile when we are happy.*
  - *I wonder why we jump when we are happy.*

What have I learned so far?

- *I have learned that playing makes me feel happy.*
- *I have learned that people laugh when they are happy.*

After Reading:

- What details did I learn about this topic?
  - *I have learned that there are many things that can make people happy.*
  - *I have learned that there are many ways you can look when you feel happy.*
- Read the book again and look for the vocabulary words.
  - *I see the word **hugs** on page 4 and the word **friends** on page 8. The other vocabulary words are found on page 14.*

Soutien de l'école à la maison pour les parents, les gardiens et les enseignants

Ce livre aide les enfants à se développer grâce à la pratique de la lecture. Voici quelques exemples de questions pour aider le lecteur ou la lectrice à développer ses capacités de compréhension. Les suggestions de réponses sont indiquées en rouge.

Avant la lecture

- De quoi ce livre parle-t-il?
  - *Ce livre parle du sentiment de la joie.*
  - *Ce livre explique à quoi ressemble la joie.*
- Qu'est-ce que je veux apprendre sur ce sujet?
  - *Je veux apprendre ce qui m'apporte de la joie.*
  - *Je veux apprendre à quoi ressemble le sentiment de la joie.*

Pendant la lecture

- Je me demande pourquoi...
  - *Je me demande pourquoi je souris quand je suis joyeux.*
  - *Je me demande pourquoi je saute quand je suis joyeux.*
- Qu'est-ce que j'ai appris jusqu'à présent?
  - *J'ai appris que jouer m'apporte de la joie.*
  - *J'ai appris que les gens rient quand ils sont joyeux.*

Après la lecture

- Nomme quelques détails que tu as retenus.
  - *J'ai appris qu'il y a plusieurs choses à faire pour apporter de la joie aux autres.*
  - *J'ai appris qu'il y a plusieurs façons de démontrer ma joie.*
- Lis le livre à nouveau et cherche les mots de vocabulaire.
  - *Je vois le mot **câlins** à la page 4 et le mot **amis** à la page 8. Les autres mots de vocabulaire se trouvent à la page 14.*

What makes me **happy**?

Qu'est-ce qui m'apporte de la **joie**?

Hugs make me happy.

Les **câlins** m’apportent de la joie.

I **smile** when I am happy.

Je **souris** quand je suis joyeux.

Playing with **friends** makes me happy.

Jouer avec mes **amis** m'apporte de la joie.

I **laugh** when I am happy.

Je **ris** quand je suis joyeux.

Helping people makes me happy.

Aider les autres m'apporte de la joie.

I jump when I am happy.

Je saute quand je suis joyeux.

What makes you happy?

Qu'est-ce qui t'apporte de la joie?

Word List / Liste de mots

Sight Words

am	people
I	what
jump	when
make	with
me	you

Mots courants

avec	qu'est-ce
je	saute
me	suis
quand	te

Words to Know
La boîte à mots

friends
amis

happy
joie

hugs
câlins

laugh
ris

smile
souris

41 Words

What makes me **happy**?

Hugs make me happy.

I **smile** when I am happy.

Playing with **friends** makes me happy.

I **laugh** when I am happy.

Helping people makes me happy.

I jump when I am happy.

What makes you happy?

51 mots

Qu’est-ce qui m’apporte de la **joie**?

Les **câlins** m’apportent de la joie.

Je **souris** quand je suis joyeux.

Jouer avec mes **amis** m’apporte de la joie.

Je **ris** quand je suis joyeux.

Aider les autres m’apporte de la joie.

Je saute quand je suis joyeux.

Qu’est-ce qui t’apporte de la joie?

My Emotions

HAPPY

Mes émotions

LA JOIE

Written by/Autrice: Amy Culliford
Designed by/Conception: Rhea Wallace
Series Development/Développement des séries: James Earley
Proofreader/ Relectrice: Ellen Rodger
Educational Consultant/Conseillère pédagogique: Marie Lemke M.Ed.

Photographs/Photographies:
Shutterstock: Juan Pablo Gonzaález: cover; Sergey Novikov: p. 1; Ami Parikh: p. 3, 14; pixelheadphoto: p. 5, 14; wavebreakmedia: p. 7, 14; ESBProfessional: p. 8, 14; TinnaPong: p. 9, 14; Africa Studio: p. 11; Monkey Business Images: p. 12; alexei_tm: p. 13

Crabtree Publishing

crabtreebooks.com 800-387-7650

Published in Canada
Publié au Canada
Crabtree Publishing
616 Welland Ave.
St. Catharines, Ontario
L2M 5V6

Published in the United States
Publié aux États-Unis
Crabtree Publishing
347 Fifth Avenue,
Suite 1402-145
New York, NY, 10016

Paperback 978-1-0398-5096-5
Ebook (pdf) 978-1-0398-5138-2
Epub 978-1-0398-5180-1

Printed in Canada/122023/CP20231116

Library and Archives Canada Cataloguing in Publication
Available at the Library and Archives Canada

Library of Congress Cataloging-in-Publication Data
Available at the Library of Congress

Word Count: 41
GRL: D
Subject: Character Ed
Genre: Nonfiction
Standard: SEL
Vocabulary Words:
friends, happy, hugs, laugh, smile

HAPPY

This book introduces early readers to the emotion of feeling happy. Simple text and vibrant images help engage children and grow a love of reading!

Books in ***My Emotions*** include:

Angry	*Calm*	*Sad*
Bored	*Happy*	*Scared*

Comte de mots : 51
NLD/GRL : préscolaire/D
Sujet : Éducation du caractère
Genre : Documentaire
Norme : ASE
Mots de vocabulaire :
amis, câlins, joie, ris, souris

LA JOIE

Ce livre présente aux nouveaux lecteurs le sentiment de la joie. Un texte simple et des images aux couleurs vives aident à motiver les enfants et à susciter l'amour de la lecture!

Les livres de la série ***Mes émotions*** comprennent :

Le calme	*L'ennui*	*La peur*
La colère	*La joie*	*La tristesse*

Teacher's Guides

Crabtree Publishing
crabtreebooks.com

ISBN 978-1-0398-5096-5
90000 >
9 781039 850965